How to Win in Life & Never Lose:

A 30-Day Devotional of Proverbial Wisdom

* Volume 1 *

Demontae A. Edmonds

HOW TO WIN IN LIFE & NEVER LOSE:
A 30-DAY DEVOTIONAL OF PROVERBIAL WISDOM

All Rights Reserved
Demontae A. Edmonds

Copyright @2018 Demontae A. Edmonds

All rights reserved. This book or any portion thereof may not be reproduced or used in any matter whatsoever without the expressed written permission of the publisher except for the use of brief quotations in a book review, social media, or scholarly journal.

Unless otherwise indicated, Scripture is taken from the King James version of the Bible.

Printed in the United States of America.

ISBN: 9781724003638

Authors Information
Demontae Edmonds
Po Box 7294
Chesapeake, VA 23324
info@f4nations.com

Table of Contents

INTRODUCTION v

DAY 1: PROPER PERSPECTIVE 1

DAY 2: THE RIGHT SELF-IMAGE 3

DAY 3: PERSONAL GROWTH 5

DAY 4: PROGRESS 7

DAY 5: TRUE-SUCCESS 9

DAY 6: A WINNING ATTITUDE 12

DAY 7: A LIFE OF SERVICE 14

DAY 8: THE GOLDEN RULE 16

DAY 9: LESSONS LEARNED 18

DAY 10: DREAMERS DON'T QUIT 20

DAY 11: ACT NOW 22

DAY 12: TEAM WORK 24

DAY 13: YOUR FINGERPRINT 26

DAY 14: THE SOUL 29

DAY 15: THE MOST POWERFUL MOTIVATOR 32

DAY 16: THINK OUTSIDE THE BOX 34

DAY 17: BE THE CHANGE YOU DESIRE 36

DAY 18: SAVE YOUR STONES 38
DAY 19: THE BEST ROPE 40
DAY 20: DON'T INSULT YOURSELF 42
DAY 21: TRUE WEALTH 45
DAY 22: ANSWER THE DOOR 48
DAY 23: WHAT MAKES YOU TICK? 51
DAY 24: EDUCATION 54
DAY 25: KEEP THE PEACE 56
DAY 26: PRODUCTIVITY 58
DAY 27: STAY HUMBLE 60
DAY 28: THE RIGHT FRIENDS, THE RIGHT WAY 62
DAY 29: FOCUS ON QUALITY 65
DAY 30: FEAR NOT 67
ABOUT THE AUTHOR 70

Introduction

Wisdom transcends time. It was needed by early man for survival and to develop advanced civilizations. Wisdom was highly prized and sought after by the Greeks and Romans alike. These classical civilizations produced great philosophers such as Socrates, Pythagoras, and Aristotle who touted the advantages of wisdom and understanding. Our current society, marked by industrial and technological achievements, still needs wisdom. Although collectively we have progressed scientifically, the fact that personal development is still requisite cannot be neglected.

"How to Win in Life & Never Lose: A 30-Day Devotional of Proverbial Wisdom" is a practical yet insightful book designed to help create a better you. The wisdom of the ages will be shared with you. Learn how to become a winner in life notable, venerated, and accomplished "sages" of ancient, pre-modern, and modern times. Allow industry leaders, star athletes, celebrity musicians, business moguls, and philosophers of old and new to become your "mentors" as you read this book. Find out some of the principles that have made them highly successful in life and in their respective disciplines and fields.

The keys in this book when read daily and put into practice will produce change within your thinking and life. As you read this book daily you will develop a winner's attitude and be challenged to take winners actions. "How to Win in Life & Never Lose: A 30-Day Devotional of Proverbial Wisdom" is an easily digestible read, applicable and valuable to the blue-collar worker, the CEO, academic, or stay at home mother. Anyone can grasp and apply these life changing insights.

Each chapter (day) is specifically written to add to the collective pool of wisdom within the book. The daily devotionals are intentionally written to be short-nuggets of truths that you can read each morning at the start of your day. As you read daily, take time to reflect upon the principle, quotation, wisdom, and reflections within each chapter.

NOW IT IS TIME TO WIN!

DAY 1

PROPER PERSPECTIVE

QUOTE

"There is no motivation like a sour pickle!"

– Benjamin Franklin

WISDOM

There are times that we all lose heart, become unfocused, and lack motivation. Often life employs the most unusual means to motivate us and push along on the path to our destiny. One of the most common and overlooked means that life uses to motivate us is the "sour pickle."

Not all pickles can be eaten.

A sour pickle is a situation or circumstance that makes us feel uncomfortable or burdened. Many fail to take action in life until they are pressed by life to do so. A few multi-millionaires have given testimony that they did not start their own business or create their own product until they were fired from a dead-end job. Promotions are often packaged in the form of problems.

Not all bad news is bad! When we receive news or change happens in our lives it may be perceived as negative. If we are going to always win in life we must continually view incidents with the proper perspective. Do you see a glass as half empty or half full? The answer is dependent upon the perspective of the beholder.

A pessimistic perspective will cause one to react to adversity. Reactions are built upon fear, anxiety, and emotions. A reactive disposition increases the changes of bad decision making. An optimistic perspective causes one to respond to adversity. A responsive disposition is based on an inner-knowing that a problem may be an opportunity in disguise.

Respond rather than react.

REFLECTIONS

1. Do you react or respond to "bad news"? If you react, what are some of the ways you can begin to respond rather than react?

2. What current situations or circumstances could be opportunities in disguise?

DAY 2

THE RIGHT SELF-IMAGE

QUOTE

"For as he thinketh in his heart; so is he."

— Solomon the Wise

WISDOM

Most, if not all, winners in life saw themselves prosperous and victorious before they achieved winner's status. What you can visualize on the inside about yourself, you can live on the outside. What you cannot see on the inside about yourself, you cannot live out in the outside world.

Winners have a positive self-image.

No boxer, desiring to be champion, enters the ring imagining themselves being knocked out. They imagine themselves standing victoriously over their opponent. If you start out any task with low self-worth and low self-esteem, then you have half-way lost the fight.

The great boxing trainer and manager Cus D'Amato knew the secret of instilling a positive self-image within the mind of boxers. World champion boxer Mike Tyson recounts an action Cus would take each night during a stay with D'Amato. Nightly, Cus would whisper into Mike's ear how great he was, how great he was going to be, and that he would be the youngest world-champion ever. "Iron" Mike Tyson found this activity strange at first, but eventually he began to believe every word spoken by his mentor. The fruit of this action was that Mike went on to become the youngest boxer to win a heavyweight boxing title and an undisputed world champion.

If you are going to think badly of anyone, don't let it be yourself.

Proverbs 23:7, "For as he thinketh in his heart; so is he." Winning in life starts with thinking of yourself the way God thinks of you – as a winner!

REFLECTIONS

1. Do others see positive attributes in you that you don't see within yourself? If so, what are they? If you are unsure then ask two other people to describe positive characteristics they see in you.

2. What are some daily exercises you can do to develop a positive self-image?

DAY 3

PERSONAL GROWTH

QUOTE

"Growth inside fuels growth outside."

– John Maxwell

WISDOM

Growth is what distinguishes living organisms from dead matter. To live is to grow. At least this should be the case with humans. Misery accompanies the man or woman who refuses to grow.

Change is good!

A winning life requires that the individual is constantly growing, evolving, and adapting to changes in environment. Any life form that fails to adapt, vitality decays and diminishes. We must esteem knowledge, wisdom, and understanding just as much as we esteem partying, fashion, or surfing social media.

Everyone can view a person's physique and physical form. The REAL you that exists on the inside cannot be seen by physical eyes. The real or inner you include your subconscious and spirit man. Both are intangible. We feed our body at least three warm meals per day and our soul languishes in starvation. Take time to invest in yourself.

The multitudes seek health, wealth, and success in the outside world. The wise man or woman knows that to win in life prosperity and wealth must first be obtained in the inner man. Surrounding yourself with things of beauty, value, and virtue help to prosper your inner man.

REFLECTIONS

1. What are you actively doing to invest in your REAL self?

2. Are you intentional about your own personal growth? If not, contemplate are three things you can start doing immediately to change this?

DAY 4

PROGRESS

QUOTE

"If there is no struggle, there is no progress."

– Frederick Douglass

WISDOM

We often think of success as living a lifestyle as depicted on Robert Leach's television show Lifestyles of the Rich and Famous. Although wealth and leisure are two signs indicative of success, there is another less welcomed sign that is often ignored ---struggle! The word struggle has a negative connotation, but its yield is often positive.

Struggle may not be your enemy!

Your enemy may be poverty, ignorance, oppression, racism, sickness, or injustice. Opposing negative forces that steal your joy and happiness produce struggle.

Struggle is the by-product of contending with opposition. When you resist mountains meant to block you, a struggle may ensue, but progress is on the other side of the mountain.

Not all struggles are bad.

Throughout history mankind has progressed morally, intellectually, and socially through great "struggles". The Civil War was instrumental in the abolishment of slavery. World War II saw the defeat of the evil plague of Nazism. The Revolutionary War enabled the end of an oppressive British monarchy's reign over the thirteen colonies.

The history of struggle is a history of progress!

REFLECTIONS

1. What past struggles in your life have produced present progress?

2. Do you avoid confrontation to "keep peace?" What confrontations in your life are avoided out of fear versus those that are necessary for progress?

DAY 5

TRUE-SUCCESS

QUOTE

"Judge your success by what you had to give up in order to get it."

– Dalai Llama

WISDOM

I once heard a story about a man who climbed to the top of a high mountain. While rejoicing and celebrating his victory he looked down and noticed all the bodies he stepped over to get to the top of mountain. Many of the individuals had been his family, friends, and colleagues. His countenance soon changed from one of jubilation to one of sorrow.

Go higher the right way and take the right people with you.

There is an old saying, "It is lonely at the top of the mountain." This is often true when individuals have achieved "success" through dubious means or inordinate ambition. Compromising one's values, morals, or ethics for the sake of gain may earn quick results but yield long term adverse consequences. Newspaper and television headlines have been filled too many times with people in position of notoriety and prestige exposed for scandalous activity.

Compromise has consequences.

Once I was traveling in a foreign land and while eating the most delicious meal I thought, "I wish my wife was here to enjoy this with me!" True success is when you can achieve your goals without losing relationships with the people dearest to you. You can truly enjoy the fruits of your labor when you have others to enjoy them with.

As we take time to prioritize our lives there should be a sandbox of people, things, and values that we refuse to compromise for the appearance of success.

Being in right relationship with God, family, and friends will ultimately make you a winner.

REFLECTIONS

1. What does success mean to you? How would it look modeled within your own life?

2. What are you willing to give up for success? What are you unwilling to give up for success?

DAY 6

A WINNING ATTITUDE

QUOTE

"You were born to win, to be a winner you must plan to win, prepare to win, and expect to win."

– Zig Zigler

WISDOM

Winners never lose, and losers never win. This oxymoron seems contradictory but expresses a great truth. Winners may lose momentarily but a winning attitude causes one to overcome loss and win again and again.

Winning is RARELY the result of luck or chance.

If you place your future in the hands of luck then your winning will be sporadic, rare, and unpredictable. Winning is resultant of proper planning and faithful execution of your plan. Champion boxers, Olympic medalist, and star athletes all train in the on and off season with the expectancy to win.

Don't take a chance leaving things to chance.

When you expect to win your thoughts, body language, conversation, and conduct should convey confidence. As a kid I would play basketball on the schoolyard basketball court. Team captains would have to pick team members often from a group of kids they didn't know. The kids with the winning look, winning attitude, and exuding confidence in their skills were always called upon first.

Planning for failure is a form of self-defeatism.

At award ceremonies musicians and actors that have newly broken into their fields are often caught off guard and shocked when presented with an award. Seasoned celebrities casually take the stage and pull from their pant or coat pocket their acceptance speech. This is because they are prepared and expect to win!

Prepare yourself to win today! Expect to win today!

REFLECTIONS

1. Do you expect to win in life or do you mentally plan for failure?
2. What is one area you really desire to win in life? What would your "acceptance" or winner's speech sound like?

DAY 7
A LIFE OF SERVICE

QUOTE

"One of the greatest diseases is to be nobody to anybody."

– Mother Theresa

WISDOM

Joy stays bottled up in the soul when we don't open our hearts and stretch out our hands to our fellow man. We become consumed and overwhelmed by our own problems when we don't take time to lend a listening ear to others in need. Our problems become smaller and less significant as we devote ourselves to give of our time, energy, and resources to helping others.

Live a life of service. Live to give.

The needs of mankind are innumerable. No individual or institution can meet all of these needs. However, we can bring comfort and solace to the life of others one soul at a time.

You may feel like a nobody, but you are somebody to somebody.

We will always undervalue ourselves when we allow our personal skills and grace to be withheld from helping others. Our true value is never realized until that value is measured by how much of a positive impact we can have on the life of others. You are valuable to others.

Many great inventions, businesses, and organizations have been started not out of the desire for wealth, but from the desire to solve a problem for mankind. Solving the needs of others, by default, positions you as a leader.

Sowing goodness into the life of others causes you to reap a harvest of peace. Mother Teresa also said, "Whenever you share love with others, you will notice that peace comes to you and them." A charitable soul is a peaceful soul.

REFLECTIONS

1. What segment of society are you called to serve?

2. Do an act of service or kindness for someone today. Write down how this act made you feel.

DAY 8

THE GOLDEN RULE

QUOTE

"Whatsoever you would have men do unto you, do ye even so to them."

– Jesus Christ

WISDOM

Our final position in life is directly correlated to how we view and treat others. Master Jesus illustriously summed this up in his teaching found in Matthew 7:12. This principle has come to be known as the Golden Rule.

See others as golden.

We must value and esteem others that we cross-paths with in the market, work place, and in society at large. It can be difficult to view others positively if we possess a negative self-view. Improving how you feel about yourself will help to improve how you feel about others.

No person is an island unto themselves. In the 20th century, it was believed that there was only seven degrees of separation between any two individuals on the earth. In the 21st century, with the advancement of technology, there may only be two or three degrees of separation between any two people on the earth. The person you treat badly may very well be connected to the person sitting in a position to open or close doors for your life.

Put your best foot forward.

Small acts of kindness and mercy go a long way in building relationships. In my own life I have witnessed people who returned years later to express gratitude in response to a kind gesture. Often, their act of appreciation came at the right time when I was in dire need of help, assistance, or a solution to a problem.

REFLECTIONS

1. Do you have a genuine interest in the well-being of others even when it is not directly to your benefit?

2. How do you desire others to treat you? Do you treat others the way you desire to be treated? If not, what are two ways you can enhance your interactions with others?

DAY 9

LESSONS LEARNED

QUOTE

"It's okay to lose: just don't lose the lesson."

— George Lucas

WISDOM

Losing is not fun. Whether one loses personally, professionally, privately, or publicly; it doesn't feel good. No one likes to lose. Losing is sometimes necessary. It gives us an opportunity to learn from our mistakes and learn new lessons.

We often get caught up in the disappointment of loss that we neglect ascertaining the lesson to be learned. In the technology and business arenas "best practices" are developed through faults, mistakes, and losses experienced at the organizational level. The lessons that we learn from situations, people, and circumstances help us to develop our own "best practices" for winning in life.

Lessons are everywhere!

Proverbs 1:20, "Wisdom crieth without, she uttereth her voice in the streets." If we look, there is wisdom and lessons to be learned all around. Studying the life of the rich man who lives in a mansion will help teach you how to get rich. Studying the life of the poor man will help you learn how not to become poor. Both the great and small things in life present lessons for us to learn.

Switch your attitude from being a loser to be a learner.

REFLECTIONS

1. What lesson(s) can be learned from a recent loss or disappointment in your life?

2. Look for lessons to be learned throughout your day from interacting with others.

DAY 10

DREAMERS DON'T QUIT

QUOTE

"A winner is a dreamer who never gives up."

— Nelson Mandela

WISDOM

Dreamers are made to win. Dreamers have a divine deposit of God-given creativity, ingenuity, and tenacity within their spirit. Dreamers are often discounted and misunderstood because they think beyond the "what is" and see "what could be."

Learn to dream again!

Abraham Lincoln had a dream to be President of the United States of America. He failed in business, loss a bid for state legislature, fiancée' died, experienced a nervous breakdown, lost a bid for Congress, lost a bid for the electorate, lost a bid for the Senate, and loss a nomination for Vice President. These are just some of the losses and hardships that he experienced in life. He would not allow failure, discouragement, or setbacks to cause his dream to be defeated. Abraham Lincoln went on to become one of the most highly regarded and remembered leaders of our time.

You are only defeated when you quit believing in your dream.

All dreamers desire to be winners. We win when our dreams come true. It takes diligence, commitment, boldness, and steadfastness to turn our dreams into reality. Dreams never die! They lay in waiting for us to exercise the proper faith to activate them. Once our dreams are activated, a divine plan sets into motion to bring all of the elements and resources needed for them to be fulfilled.

REFLECTIONS

1. What dreams have you buried in your heart due to disappointment?

2. Take time to write down 3 dreams in your heart that you have not acted upon. How you can start today to pursue these dreams into fulfillment?

DAY 11

ACT NOW

QUOTE

"You have to act, and act now."

– Larry Ellison

WISDOM

Winners are doers. Actions gives proof to your faith and belief that you will win at whatever you set out to do in life. Many great visions, ideas, and businesses are buried in the cemetery with people who failed to act.

The cemetery is full of great ideas.

There is a common saying, "Talk is cheap!" Talk only produces fruit if it is connected to action. Don't delay stepping out of the boat of inaction by looking at your present circumstances. Rarely does every factor in your life and environment line up perfectly.

Ecclesiastes 11:4, "He that observes the wind will not sow; and he that regards the clouds shall not reap." If we wait for every circumstance within the affairs of our life to be perfect before we take action, then we will forever be stagnant. Don't allow the clouds of life to cause you to remain in a house of inaction.

Failure to act today results in regret tomorrow.

At one time I was a subscriber to a widely circulated business magazine. The magazine would highlight successful minority entrepreneurs and business start-ups. Many of the featured stories were of individuals who were down on their luck, unemployed, and/or struggling to "make ends meet." These individuals would go on to become multi-millionaire business owners. I began to take note, regardless of the circumstances, they all had one thing in common. They stepped out on faith and acted upon the desire within their heart to succeed.

"Don't put off until tomorrow what you can do today."
– Benjamin Franklin

REFLECTIONS

1. When it rains do you grab an umbrella and brave the storm? Or do you allow circumstances to rain on your parade and stop your plans?

2. What task have you been putting off until tomorrow that you can complete today?

DAY 12

TEAM WORK

QUOTE

"Great things in business are never done by one person. They are done by a team of people."

– Steve Jobs

WISDOM

There is nothing like sharing a vision with others, working toward that vision, and celebrating its realization together. Throughout history there have been notable leaders who brought about great change in society. These leaders were surrounded by individuals who shared many of the same goals and vision.

Team work makes the dream work!

Synergy happens when you bring the right team members together. You can accomplish more with the help of others than you can working at a task alone. Also, often it takes less effort and sacrifice, at the individual level to produce great results when a team is involved.

If you have a dream, it takes a team.

Life sends to us team members to help us win in life. A spouse, a brother, a sister, a friend, a co-worker, or associate...they may all be your team member. We must identify those individuals in our life who are called to operate in our periphery. In contrast, there are individuals who need our partnership and we need theirs to arrive at our destination of destiny.

Your team doesn't need a name just a common purpose.

REFLECTION

1. What goals in your life require teamwork?

2. Identify individuals personally and professionally that you can partner with for mutual advancement.

DAY 13

YOUR FINGERPRINT

QUOTE

"I've come to believe that each of us has a personal calling that's as unique as a fingerprint."

– Oprah Winfrey

WISDOM

Every advanced technology product that leaves a factory and production line comes with an owner's manual. The owner's manual gives instructions, details, and insights on the product's purpose, proper maintenance, and use.

The Divine Creator predestined and predesigned purpose into our DNA before we were born into the earth. Coded within our divine design is our "personal calling" or vocation in which we are purposed, graced, and preprogrammed to operate. We all have a calling. Whether great or small, your calling brings fulfillment and joy in your life.

Your calling is unique to you just like your fingerprint! No one can do what you do the way you do it!

Many have obtained advanced degrees and notable professional careers. After years of working in their respective disciplines they discovered that their profession brought little joy or sense of fulfillment to their life. They gained wealth and acclaim at the expense of compromising their true purpose in life.

Working in a field that you enjoy, one that impacts the lives of others, and that adds to your own personal growth gives you a great sense of purpose and worth.

No one can find your calling for you. Life will take you down a road of self-discovery where it will be revealed to you over time. For some, such as Mozart, life reveals their divine calling at a rather early age. For others their personal calling may come after a season of hardship, a season of searching for answers, or a divine encounter with the Creator.

No matter what age or season in life you discover your personal calling- EMBRACE IT!

REFLECTIONS

1. What is your personal calling in life? What audience or demographic of society are you called to empower, inspire, impact, or influence?

2. What are you doing to pursue your personal calling? If nothing, start today!

DAY 14

THE SOUL

QUOTE

"Grow your soul and reach your goals."

– Demontae Edmonds

WISDOM

Authors Jack Canfield and Mark Victor Hansen highlighted the need for the soul to receive inspiration and encouragement in their Chicken Soup for the Soul book series. We are all three-part beings: spirit, soul, and body. The soul consists of our mind, will, and emotions.

3 John 1:2, "Beloved, I wish above all things that thou mayest prosper and be in health, even as thy soul prospers."

Prosper your soul, prosper your life!

Your mind includes your thoughts, reasoning, and cognitive faculties. It gives you the ability to make sound and wise decisions that help you win in life.

Will-power is needed for winning in life. A strong-willed person will rarely quit or throw in the towel. Will-power gives one the fortitude to overcome obstacles and hurdles.

Your emotions dictate your feelings, mood, and response to situations, people, and places. Unresolved soul issues can lead to emotional instability. Unstable emotions can rob you of happy, peace, joy and fruitful relationships. Also, it will make one indecisive.

A wounded soul can be a source of physical ailment and sickness. I have seen many recuperate from an illness only to immediately get sick again and again. This phenomenon often is due to unhealed trauma or soul wounds.

Proverbs 18:14, "The spirit of man will sustain his infirmity; but a wounded spirit who can bear?"

Drawing closer to God, counseling, Eye Movement Desensitization & Reprocessing (EMDR), and inner-healing sessions are some of the effective ways to bring healing to the soul.

REFLECTIONS

1. How have past events affected your emotional stability and emotional maturity?

2. What action(s) can you take to improve the condition of your soul?

DAY 15

THE MOST POWERFUL MOTIVATOR

QUOTE

"For love is heaven, and heaven is love."

— Sir Walter Scott

WISDOM

There is no greater motivator and inspiring force than that of love. Love has a magnetic pull that can both draw people to you. It can also attract you to others.

Where there is love, there is sacrifice.

Love colors the soul, warms the heart, and frees the intellect to reach its highest heights. When love is bound, the heart and mind is held captive to lesser forces. Fear, doubt, worry, anxiety, and unbelief are opposing forces to love; but they are inferior in strength and influence. To be full of love is to eradicate fear and anxiety from one's inner life.

Love is an action word.

Real love requires action. A gift, kind word, friendly gesture, or act of mercy all are acts that demonstrate love. Many fail to experience love because they have not first learned to give it out. You reap what you sow – learn to sow love and reap a harvest of goodness.

REFLECTIONS

1. Take time to show love to someone who needs it today!

2. Appreciate someone who has consistently shown you love.

DAY 16

THINK OUTSIDE THE BOX

QUOTE

"If everyone is thinking alike, then somebody isn't thinking."

— General George S. Patton

WISDOM

Innovators and history-makers are not afraid to think outside of the box. Thought leaders become pioneers and leaders of men. People who think outside the box become "thought leaders" within society.

It is often easier to try to fit in or "go with the flow." Psychology teaches us that it is natural for us to desire acceptance. Behaving, thinking, or expressing one's self differently than the current popular stream can cause an individual to feel alienated or ostracized. Boldness is required to be an out of the box thinker.

If you don't think outside the box, then you will live inside a box of limitation.

Every period within history mankind has been presented with new challenges and obstacles that required creative solutions. For example, the Industrial Age saw the rise of great factories and large-scale production of goods. Huge sprawling populations begin to centralize in and around major industrial centers. The problems of overcrowding and urbanization had to be addressed by a new breed of civil engineers, city planners, and real estate developers.

Your thinking outside the box frees someone else from their box. Foreword and free-thinking cause you to become the solution to someone else's problem. Be a problem-solver!

REFLECTION

1. What boxes have you allowed to imprison your thoughts?

2. Are you afraid to challenge the status quo? If so, how can you overcome this fear?

DAY 17

BE THE CHANGE YOU DESIRE

QUOTE

"Be the change you want to see in the world."

— Mahatma Ghandi

WISDOM

Complainers are grumblers, moaners, and nitpickers; they are seldom agents of change. It takes very little skill or intelligence to find what's wrong in life, society or the world. In contrast, it requires strength of character and resolve to be an agent of change.

Change starts with YOU!

A pastor in Illinois shared his testimony of how his marriage was rocky and there was constant disagreement and division. As he was praying to God about changing his wife, he heard God say, "You are worrying about me changing her. You have not allowed me to change you." Thus, begun a personal journey of this pastor thinking and speaking positively and faith-filled words each day. Eventually, he noticed that the marriage had improved, and his wife had changed. He was no longer trying to change her but focused on changing his own behaviors and it ultimately his actions affected her.

Change is contagious!

President Barack Obama campaigned on the slogan, "Change You Can Count On!" Many have been disappointed by broken political promises. The only change that you can count on is the change you initiate in your own life. This is the change with which the universe holds you accountable.

Refusal to change is refusal to progress.

REFLECTIONS

1. Identify the area of your life that has the highest priority for change. What are you doing to help cultivate that change within yourself?

2. Have you hindered your own progress in life by refusing to change?

DAY 18

SAVE YOUR STONES

QUOTE

"You will never reach your destination if you stop to throw stones at every dog that barks."

– Sir Winston Churchill

WISDOM

We are all born into earth with limited time and energy to accomplish our mission in life. These resources must be properly stewarded. The proper usage of energy and time creates results. Wasted energy equals inefficiency.

There are legitimate problems and concerns that require our attention. There exist situations and issues that may pop up on our radar but may not require our attention. As the saying goes, "Where there is smoke there is fire." It is not purposeful for us to put out every fire. When you put out the wrong fires you get burned and come out smelling like smoke.

When our family goes on long-distance road trips there is often new scenery. Our small children always take note of things of interest along the sides of the road. While peering out of their car windows they will shout, "Mom, Dad, can we stop and see that!". Often, it's a landmark or sight that would grab a child's attention. We acknowledge their excitement but also explain that we cannot stop to visit every sight because it would delay our arrival at our destination.

Don't be delayed by distractions. Choose your battles wisely. Some battles, even if you win, you lose because they drain you of precious energy, and rob you of precious time.

REFLECTION

1. Identify and avoid at least one distraction on today.

2. What has been a distraction for you in different seasons of your life? Why?

DAY 19

THE BEST ROPE

QUOTE

"Prayer is the rope that pulls God and man together."

– Billy Graham

WISDOM

Religions may differ in their cosmology, adherence, and methodologies of devotion. Prayer is a foundational practice that most religions hold in common. Although prayer is for the religious, its true purpose isn't religious, but rather relational.

Prayer is about communication. Man communicating with a God who desires to reciprocate.

Mogul business woman Oprah Winfrey shares the story of how she desired an acting role in the movie The Color Purple. Two months after auditioning for the role she had not received a call from the casting director. She became discouraged and begin to cry. Oprah turned her thoughts and heart God-ward. She began to pray and sing "I SURRENDER ALL." At that moment she received a phone call from movie producer Steven Spielberg who offered a role in the movie.

Prayer displays your dependency upon a higher power.

Our weaknesses are exchanged for Heaven's strength when we pray. In prayer, burdens that have weighted down our soul and countenance are lifted. Prayer requires no formality, only sincerity of the heart.

Prayer is honesty with God about your need for help, wisdom, and guidance.

REFLECTIONS

1. Have you tried the best rope [prayer]? If so, is it time to add this back into your daily routine?

2. How do you view prayer? Do you view it as a religious activity or a relational action?

DAY 20

DON'T INSULT YOURSELF

QUOTE

"Don't compare yourself with anyone in this world, if you do so, you are insulting yourself."

– Bill Gates

WISDOM

It is a natural human tendency to compare one's self to others. In childhood teachers indirectly create an atmosphere of contrast and competition within the education system. Children also learn from their parents and other adults how to judge and size up other individuals based on their dress, speech, appearance, ethnicity, and other external factors. By the time that one becomes an adult, thoughts about personal strengths and weaknesses based on comparison have already been established.

The grass isn't always greener on the other side.

Many are desirous to become a celebrity, entertainer or athlete. One Grammy award winning singer, songwriter, and pop icon made the comment, "A person would have to be crazy to want to be a celebrity entertainer, just look at my life!" From the outside looking in this young lady had it all - beauty, fame, and fortune. Truthfully, she had many life challenges that accompanied her stardom that caused her great heart-ache and frustration.

You are different for a reason.

Why is it an insult to compare yourself to others? You were uniquely designed for a unique purpose. When you compare yourself to others you limit your potential by allowing the abilities or achievements of others to serve as your measuring stick. Also, while you may able to clearly see people's strengths, it may be difficult to see their inadequacies.

The Ugly Duckling by Danish poet Hans Christian Andersen tells the story of a young duckling who suffered loneliness and depression because of being bullied and teased for his appearance. None of the other ducks desired his company, whenever possible highlighting his differences from them. This duckling admired a flock of swans for their beauty. He knew that he could never join with them. One day he reluctantly joins the flock, and when he looks at his reflection in the water he realizes that he was never a duckling, but a swan the entire time.

Your beauty isn't realized until you begin to fulfill your purpose in the earth. Winners don't compare themselves to others, instead they reach their individual full potential and work to complete others.

REFLECTIONS

1. What events from your childhood affect how you view yourself in relationship to others?

2. Write down three things that make you uniquely designed.

DAY 21

TRUE WEALTH

QUOTE

"True wealth is not measured in money or status or power. It is measured in the legacy that we leave behind for those we love and those we inspire."

– Cesar Chavez

WISDOM

For many the word "wealth" provokes thoughts of the once popular television show Lifestyles of the Rich and Famous hosted by Robin Leach. Monetary riches are merely a limited form or realm of wealth. Wealth is not limited to the material realm or physical realm.

To be wealthy is to be prosperous, at peace, and healthy.

A gentleman named Carl shared with me a story about a rich man that he encountered while working on his job.

Carl worked for a local television company as a cable installer. He was sent to a certain man's home to setup a new cable connection. The owner of the house laid on a couch beside a table full of money.

Carl questioned inquired about why there was so much money just sitting out in the open. The homeowner, an older man, explained that he was a multi-millionaire and had more money than he would ever need in life. Also, he had two children, both unfit and unworthy to gain his inheritance. Furthermore, he stated that the money had been a source of trouble and stress for him.

Money can buy almost anything, but it isn't everything. Many are miserable because they are working only for themselves and not building a legacy.

Many have worked toward a goal their entire life and died in grief not having obtained their desire. You may not be able to obtain the wealth, status, influence or social change in life that you desire. Don't allow a lack of money to make you feel like a loser. There are other intangible gems such character, faith, wisdom, and lessons learned that can passed on to others. knowledge and resources that you pass down to others allows you to live and win vicariously through future generations.

Great leaders leave great legacies. Winners setup those that follow in their footsteps to win in life.

REFLECTIONS

1. Have you been intentional about leaving a legacy for future generations?

2. What are some tangible assets and intangible values that you can leave for future generations?

DAY 22

ANSWER THE DOOR

QUOTE

"If you're offered a seat on a rocket ship, don't ask what seat! Just get on!"

– Sheryl Sandberg

WISDOM

As a kid it was guaranteed on a Saturday morning that there would be random knocks on the front door. Standing at the door would be a neighbor, the mailman, salesman, someone from one of the local churches seeking converts, or another kid desiring me to come outside and play. My father often instructed me to ignore the knock at the door and to be quiet as if no one was in the house. There were some visitors to be avoided.

There is one visitor not to be avoided when he knocks at the door of your life - opportunity.

When opportunity knocks, open the door!

We don't know when opportunity will knock, or how the opportunity will look. We do know when opportunity appears one must take advantage of it. There is no estimation when it will prevent itself again. Some opportunities only come once in life.

Ecclesiastes 9:11 says, "I returned, and saw under the sun, that the race is not to the swift, nor the battle to the strong, neither yet bread to the wise, nor yet riches to men of understanding, nor yet favor to men of skill; but time and chance happens to them all."

Timing + chance = opportunity. One can only take advantage of time and chance through proper preparation. Winners are not always those born with the best abilities. Practice, study, discipline, and consistency in your field of endeavor (sports, entertainment, business, etc.) prepare you for when opportunity knocks. Failure to prepare is equally as foolish as failing to open the door when opportunity knocks.

NBA Legend Michael Jordan was denied a spot on his high school's varsity basketball team during his sophomore year due to his lack of height. During the summer, he trained daily, consistently, and intensely. Daily he would work on his dribble, jump shot, and free throw shot. Preparation positioned him to walk through the door of opportunity the next year of his high school's basketball season.

Prepare for a knock at the door. Expect the knock at the door. OPEN THE DOOR!

REFLECTIONS

1. Do you open, ignore, or close the door when opportunity knocks?

2. What are you doing to prepare yourself for when opportunity knocks?

DAY 23

WHAT MAKES YOU TICK?

QUOTE

"I actually think better when I'm in high heels."

– Theresa May

WISDOM

Winning in life involves performing at peak levels. Maximizing your potential has great reward. One of the greatest rewards is a feeling of accomplishment, self-worth, and self-actualization. Abraham Maslow's, his 1943 paper "A Theory of Human Motivation", describes human's hierarchy of needs. At the top of the hierarchy of human development is self-actualization.

A person becomes self-actualized when they reach their highest level of potential in life. For many to reach this level they must first find what makes them tick. A study of successful and notable people reveals that many of them have quirks. These quirks or peculiarities help them to clear their minds, function at a higher level of intelligence, and/or increase in productivity.

Theresa May, Prime Minister of the United Kingdom, says that wearing high heels help her to think better. This may sound trivial, but many public speakers know that nice attire increases your confidence while delivering presentations. I once worked with a brilliant and successful marketer. Every day he would drink three cups of coffee. Jokingly he would exclaim, "One cup for the body, one cup for the mind, and one cup for the soul." Coffee was a crutch, maybe with placebo effect, to get him stirred up to work at his best pace.

Inventor Thomas Edison said that "Genius is one percent inspiration and ninety-nine percent perspiration." He credited many of his inventions being the result of hard work and long hours. An equally ingenious inventor, Nikola Tesla, credited many of his discoveries to revelatory and visionary experiences. These experiences were often almost spiritual in nature. Two inventors but two different methodologies. Both inventors had to find what made them tick and to harness the power of their own individuality.

It is vital that you find what make you ticks. For some it may be a morning ritual or routine. For others it may be wearing a certain color suit. For another it may be having photos of family or loved ones on your work desk.

REFLECTIONS

1. What quirks in your life may be unique triggers to help increase your productivity in life?

2. What are two things that make you "tick"? Are they necessary or unnecessary in your life?

DAY 24

EDUCATION

QUOTE

"Education is what remains after one has forgotten what one has learned in school."

– Albert Einstein

WISDOM

Life presents opens doors and opportunities but too often we are ill prepared to walk in the doors and take advantage of the opportunities. A lack of education diminishes our ability to seize the moment. Education gives us a strategic leverage in life by enhancing our knowledge and skill sets.

Never stop being a student!

A science school teacher once told me, "I'm a teacher, but I will never stop being a student." Education is not just something that we pursue to obtain a degree or certificate. It should be a lifelong endeavor. Education can come in many forms: formal, informal, and non-formal. If we desire to better ourselves, then we should be intentional about increasing our abilities and skills.

In the Bible, the character Daniel is recognized as a major prophet. It is often overlooked that it was not just his spiritual abilities alone that gained him promotion, favor, and audience with kings and emperors. Daniel 1:17 says, "God gave them knowledge and skill in all learning and wisdom; and Daniel had understanding in all visions and dreams."

"Some know the value of education by having it. I know its value by not having it" – Frederick Douglas

Education gives you leverage in life for promotions and advancement.

REFLECTIONS

1. What free platforms can you use to enrich your current level of education?

2. Do others view you as educated? How does this perception of you from others decrease or increase your chances for promotion and advancement?

DAY 25

KEEP THE PEACE

QUOTE

"There is no right way to argue."

– Aesop

WISDOM

Winning an argument can be likened to winning a battle but losing the war. The person who loses an argument often will feel a sense of resentment toward the person who bested them. The winner may feed their ego or gain a sense of accomplishment, but rarely will strengthen friendships or accomplish goals through arguing.

Conflict is only good if it is constructive.

Most arguments can be avoided. Responding rather than reacting. Listening with the intent to understand the other party's position and concerns. Asking questions rather than railing accusations. These are just some of the measures that can be taken to avoid unnecessary conflicts.

Be intentional about keeping the peace.

An argumentative person is never a joyful person or a person at peace. Often there exists unresolved turmoil within an individual's soul that causes them to be easily agitated. When I was a child my martial arts instructor shared with me, "Avoid loud and aggressive people." At a young age he had given me a formula for avoiding individuals with a high propensity for unfruitful confrontation.

Transparency, clear, and consistent communications helps to build relational capital with family, friends, coworkers, and acquaintances. This relational capital reduces the risk of hostile disagreements as each party is concerned the mutual interest of the other. Relationships may be easily formed, but it takes work to cultivate them.

REFLECTIONS

1. Do you find yourself frequently arguing or engaged in arguments? What unresolved internal issues from your own life may contribute to this characteristic?

2. Avoid unneeded conflict by avoiding individuals prone to strife.

DAY 26

PRODUCTIVITY

QUOTE

"It is the idle man who is the miserable man"

– Benjamin Franklin

WISDOM

There is a well-known saying that "Misery loves company!" I believe the company that misery keeps is idleness and laziness. Misery just doesn't happen. It is often the by-product of inaction, poor time-management, and a negative attitude. A miserable life is a bitter life.

You don't have to keep misery company.

Productivity causes us to win in life. God created us to be producers. God's command to Adam and Eve was for them to in Genesis 1:28, "Be fruitful and multiply." In layman's terms God told them, "Be productive!" We should always be setting goals and achieving accomplishments.

Those with poor time management have low productivity in life. They want to enjoy the good life but are inconsistent in the actions and behaviors required for such. Money can be recovered, time cannot. Today value your time just as much as you value the money in your pocket. Time pays if it is used correctly.

Time waits for no man.

Let idleness become your enemy. Let rest become your friend. Idleness is the wasting of time. Resting is the break from activities in order to refresh and recuperate in an effort to be more productive when resuming one's activities. God rested from His work only AFTER He had actually worked and completed what He set out to accomplish.

Genesis 2:2, "And he rested on the seventh day from all of his work."

REFLECTION

1. Do you map out in advance how you will spend your time each day?

2. Which unproductive activities consume your time? Can you eliminate these activities from your daily or weekly routine?

DAY 27
STAY HUMBLE

QUOTE

"The bigger the head, the bigger the headache."

– M.K.O. Abiola

WISDOM

The first sin recorded in the Bible is the pride that led to Lucifer's fall from grace. Pride is as ancient as the notorious former archangel and prehistoric man. Pride has been the great stumbling block and deceiver of many great men and women.

Proverbs 16:18, "Pride goes before destruction, and a haughty spirit before a fall."

Pride and arrogance have the cunning ability to blind the heart and deceive the mind. There is a saying among celebrities and accomplished athletes alike, "Don't believe your own hype!" Big headaches follow "getting the big head." Drama, problems, and conflicts often follow the prideful heart. Pride abides in the heart where insecurity exists.

Skill, abilities, and accomplishments may make an individual great. When greatness is complemented by the character attribute of humility – a person becomes exceptional. Humility causes one to keep their head low and out of harm's way.

Winners stay humble!

REFLECTIONS

1. Does success or achievements make you feel accomplished or prideful?

2. In your life, what are some negative situations that can be avoided by humble behavior or responses?

DAY 28

THE RIGHT FRIENDS, THE RIGHT WAY

QUOTE

"Reading good books implants good ideas in the mind, develops good aspirations, and leads to the cultivation of good friends."

– Masutatsu Oyama

WISDOM

It has been said that if a person lived life with at least one true friend, that person has lived a rich life. The right relationships are necessary for winning in life. Friendships enhance life. It is of great worth to be able to share, grow, learn, relax, play, work, and celebrate with others whose company and presence you enjoy.

Some have attempted to win friends through shallow means. Relationships not built around a meaningful purpose, or a common goal are often short term and seasonal. We often become frustrated with the how and when these relationships end but fail to realize many of them were not built upon the proper foundation.

Ideas attract people.

Wrong thinking will attract wrong relationships. Right thinking will attract the right relationships. We attract who we are and what we value. Reading and exposing ourselves to teachings that exalt principles, values, and ideas that promote morality, prosperity, good deeds, and well-being develops our inner consciousness. Our consciousness attracts those of other like consciousness. Those who hold the same ideas and values of high esteem.

Let the Law of Attraction bring the right friends into your life.

There may exist differences of opinions and disagreements between friends. Ideas and values are glues that can bond people together. Shared vision and ideologies can bridge individuals despite different backgrounds, upbringings, ethnicities, education levels, and experience levels.

Take time today to water the seeds of good ideas within your soul and positive aspirations in your heart. A better you will spring up and new friends will sprout forth in your life.

REFLECTIONS

1. What ideas or ideologies do you hold in great value? How does these positively or negatively impact your relationships?

2. What good aspirations are you pursuing? Has this limited or enhanced relationships in your life?

DAY 29

FOCUS ON QUALITY

QUOTE

"Better a little which is well done, then a great deal imperfectly."

– Plato

WISDOM

What do Tiger Woods, Beyoncé, Bill Gates, and Michael Jordan all have in common? Though they may have many talents, they are all recognized and celebrated for one notable talent. Tiger Woods is applauded for his golfing ability, Michael Jordan for his basketball skills, Bill Gates his tech business savvy, and Beyoncé for her musical abilities.

Make the main thing the main thing!

Michael Jordan played baseball well, but he is not remembered for his accomplishments on the baseball field.

We identify him with the area of his greatness - basketball. A person who dabbles in many skills, rather than becoming proficient in one is said to be a "Jack of all trades, master of none." These individuals often become busy-bodies doing much but accomplishing little.

You may do 100 things well, but only one great. Discovering what you do great, develop your talent in that area, and display that talent to the world. Passion is dissipated when not tied into a pursuit. Where there is passion, there is energy and motivation. Many lack motivation and the energy to win because they haven't put their hand to the plow in the area of their proficiency.

Quality over quantity.

When we are "spread too thin" in our actions and doings it is difficult to cultivate a spirit of excellence in our endeavors. A spirit of excellence causes one's behavior, words, skills, and actions to shine. Quality of action and excellence go hand and hand.

Today find what you do well and improve your quality of action in that activity.

REFLECTIONS

1. What are two things that you do very well?
2. Have you focused your time and energy into maximizing your potential in the things that you do well?

DAY 30

FEAR NOT

QUOTE

"As a rule, men worry more about what they can't see than what they can"

– Julius Caesar

WISDOM

"Don't Worry, Be Happy" are the lyrics and title to the popular hit song by musician Bob McFerrin. These lyrics contain a great truth. Worry is the enemy to our faith. Worry is the inverse of faith. The soul full of faith believes for a positive income and favor in all situations. Worry is a belief as well. It is a belief in negative outcomes or results. Many exercise the power of belief, just in the wrong direction, in the negative direction.

Fear not.

There are legitimate concerns in life that require us to take heed and caution. However, we often stress over "what ifs" and possibilities that never appear in reality. This is likened unto shadow boxing, fighting an imaginary opponent. Don't worry about what may happen, when you can focus your energy on what is present before you.

Don't "psych" yourself out.

I remember being told the story of the lady who tremendously worried that she might have cancer. She went to doctors multiple times complaining that she had all the symptoms of a deadly cancer. Each time the doctors would assure her that she was cancer free and sent her own with an encouraging word that nothing was wrong with. Eventually, cancer did ravish her body and she died very suddenly. Could this woman have lived a long prosperous life, or did she literally worry herself to death?

Fear and worry attract negative energy.

Sometimes no news is good news. Don't go and invent negative news. Many who suffered disappointment and trauma during childhood are used to "drama" being their norm.

Replace your fear with faith!

REFLECTIONS

1. What type of circumstances trigger fear in your life and why?

2. What fear-based responses can you replace with faith-based responses?

About the Author

Demontae Edmonds is an international speaker and workshop presenter. He has traveled throughout the United States, Europe, Asia, Africa, and the Caribbean sharing messages of hope, inspiration, leadership, and encouragement. As a highly sought out voice of wisdom he has ministered to kings, CEOs, government officials, and community leaders.

Demontae has been the special guest on many regional, national, and international television and radio broadcasts. In the U.S.A these include TBN "Praise the Lord", Oracle TV, CBN News, Atlanta Live, Spirit Fuel TV, iHeart Radio, Faith USA Network, Total Christian Television, IMPACT Network and God TV. In the U.K. these include BIG HITS Radio, Premier UK Radio, Turning Point Intl, & UCB UK Radio. Overseas broadcast includes Power Vision TV (India), Cable Vision TV (Africa), Empowerment Zone (Turks & Caicos), LATENA Radio (Ghana), FM Love Radio (Nigeria), and Cable Vision TV (Africa).

Demontae is proudly the husband of Jessica. Together they have three beautiful small children.

In addition to "How to Win in Life & Never Lose: A 30 Day Devotional of Proverbial Wisdom", he is the author of "Grab Hold of Your Miracle: 10 Keys to Experiencing Supernatural Miracles", "Discerning of Spirits: 7 Dimensions of Revelation."

CONTACT

Website: www.f4nations.com

Contact: info@f4nations.com

Mail: Freedom 4 the Nations

   Po Box 7294, Chesapeake, VA 23324

Made in the
USA
Middletown, DE